For Those Who Read This Book to Children

SUNLIGHT introduces young children to science and aims at learning needs.

Children learn through their own actions; their own experimentation and discovery. Book questions, by inviting child questions, encourage active thinking and doing.

When a young child is filled with feelings and thoughts in terms of himself and his immediate environment, few generalizations are meaningful. Facts removed from his immediate senses are too remote for him to understand.

The information and action in this book help build a feeling of mastery within the young child's own perceptual world. Among the many experiences in day care and nursery school, these seemed to best meet the children's emotional and cognitive needs for learning.

When you read and "do" this book with a child, respond to the child's feelings and thinking and give your warmest support to his own learning.

S.C.

Sunlight

by Sally Cartwright
illustrated by Marylin Hafner

Coward, McCann & Geoghegan, Inc.   New York

General Editor: Margaret Farrington Bartlett

Text copyright © 1974 by Sally Cartwright
Illustrations copyright © 1974 by Marylin Hafner

SBN: GB-698-30540-X
SBN: TR-698-20288-0

Library of Congress Catalog Card Number: 73-88022
Printed in the United States of America
03207

To the Children and Parents
of the
Watertown Cooperative Nursery School

Do you ever wake early when the day is starting?
Outside it begins to get light.

Daylight comes over the towns
and the hills.
Light comes to your street,
to your house, to your room.

Soon you see the sun itself.
It is far away,
but it is so bright
it will hurt your eyes
if you look at it for long.

Without sunlight, the night is dark.
Daytime is filled with light from the sun.

Sunlight can shine through some things.
Can it shine through window glass?
Look and see.

Can it shine through water?
Hold a glass of water in sunlight,
and see for yourself.

Can sunlight shine through ice?
Hold an ice cube in the sunlight and find out.

Stand in the sunlight.
Look for your shadow.
It is shady and dark.
You make a shadow
because the sunlight
cannot go through you.

12

Can you find other shadows?

A fence?

A tree?

A cloud?

A tricycle?

A house?

When a cloud hides the sun,
sunlight cannot shine through the cloud.

So the cloud makes a shadow.
It is shady and dark, like your shadow.

Find a room where the sun
is shining through a window.
Hold a small mirror
in the sunlight.
Your mirror will catch and send
a bright bit of sunlight
to the wall of the room.

When light touches a shiny surface,
it bounces off again
the way you bounce a ball.
This is called reflection.
Your mirror reflects the light which touches it.

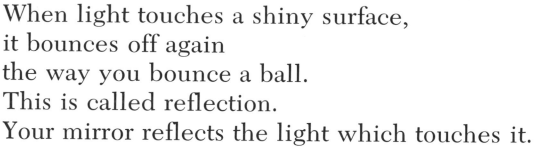

Wiggle your mirror
to help you find the sunlight
it sends to the wall.
Can you find it?
Can you make it go where you like?

Sunlight often flashes from shiny things.
Watch a stream, or a lake, or the sea.
Water reflects the sunlight.
It sparkles on the waves.

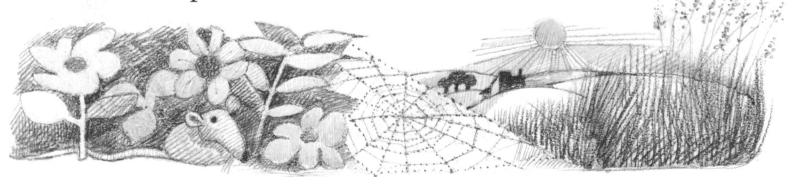

In early morning
sunlight shines on the wet grass.
The tiny drops of dew
reflect the sunlight.
They can make a spider web
look like threads of silver.

Sunlight can make rainbow colors.

Mix soapy water in a bowl.
Put the bowl in sunlight.
Blow bubbles in the bowl with a straw.
What colors can you see?

Put a bowl filled with clear water in the sunlight.

Hold a small mirror under the water.

You can catch the sunlight under the water and reflect it onto a white sheet of paper held nearby.

Wiggle your mirror. Do you see the light making colors that move on the paper?

You can see rainbow colors
in a fine spray of water in the sunlight.
A garden hose, a fountain, a lawn sprinkler
can make good spray.

To see the rainbow, stand so the sun shines
from behind you as you watch the spray.

Light from the sun
helps leafy plants and trees grow.
Put a small green potted plant
in a dark closet.
After a while it will die in the dark
unless it has sunlight again.

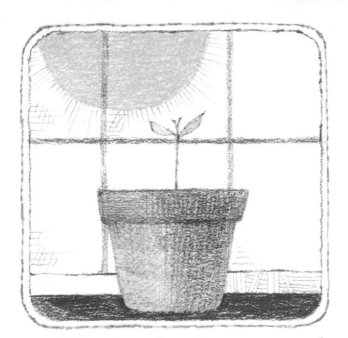 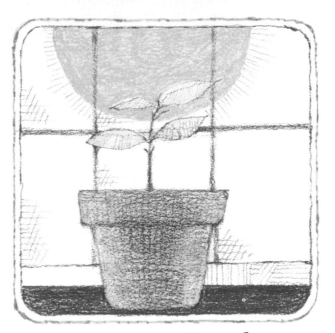

Watch what happens when you put a growing plant
on the windowsill in sunlight.

After a while the leaves will turn
toward the light. The green leaves use the sunlight
to help the plant grow.

The sun not only sends us light,
it sends us heat.

In summertime sunlight feels hot!
Sometimes you go barefoot.
You wear shorts.
You stay in the shade
or take a swim to keep cool.

When the sun is shining,
go outdoors.
Hold your hand in the sunlight.
Does it feel warm?

Even on a cold winter day,
standing in the sunlight makes you warm.

Summer days are long.
There is more light and warmth.
But when winter comes,
the days are short and cold.
You put on your warmest clothes
when you go out.

After winter is over,
the sunlight warms the air and land and water.
Walk out in the early spring.

See what warm sunlight can do.
It melts the ice and snow.
It dries the puddles.

It turns the mud to dry dirt.
You can scuff it into dust.

Spring sunlight warms the ponds.
Frogs and fish and turtles lay their eggs.

28 Chipmunks and squirrels and rabbits have their babies now.

Flowers and leaf buds open
in the long, warm days of sunlight.

New leaves grow on the bushes and trees.
Go outdoors and see for yourself:

29

The whole countryside is changed to green
in the light and warmth of the summer sun.

At the end of each day evening comes,
and the night is shady and dark,
like your own shadow.
This is a good time to sleep
and be ready to discover
a new day
of sunlight and warmth.

31

About the Author

To sail a sloop 500 miles down the coast of New England single-handed is quite a feat, but to own and sail one's own (homemade) boat at the age of six seems even more impressive. Sally Cartwright has done both, in addition to having sailed small craft on the Red Sea, the Ganges River, and both U.S. coasts.

Sally Cartwright has been teaching young children about science for many years and is the author of *The Tide* and *Animal Homes* in the Science Is What and Why series. Mrs. Cartwright lives with her family in Cambridge, Massachusetts.

About the Artist

Marylin Hafner studied at Pratt Institute and the School of Visual Arts in New York. She has worked in many art-related fields, doing design and art for advertising, designing textiles, and, of course, illustrating children's books.